Alone Together

For
Joseph
and
Amalie

"It's hard to explain difficult times to young children.
I wanted to write a book to comfort those children who feel lonely,
let them know that we are all in this together, and give them
hope that other days will be different."

Julia Seal

It isn't a normal
kind of day.

The sun is up, the birds are out,

but everybody's indoors.

Mom is busy working from home.

Dad says I can't go on the swings.

Grandma isn't coming to visit.

It's just me and Stripy.

It's a strange
sort of day.

The streets are empty, the world is quiet.

Everybody's indoors.

Dad says I can't play
with my friends.

Auntie Jane can't drive
me to soccer practice.

Grandad's not coming
for Sunday lunch.

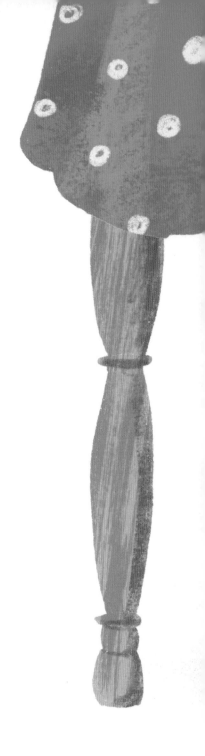

It's just me and Rabbit.

If only I could go to
the playground...

If only I could go
to soccer...

Maybe I'll build a tower.

Maybe I'll build a den.

Perhaps I'll write a story.

Perhaps I'll read a book.

I miss my friends.

Maybe I'll
draw him
a picture!

Maybe I'll
write her
a message!

Perhaps I'll show her my magic trick!

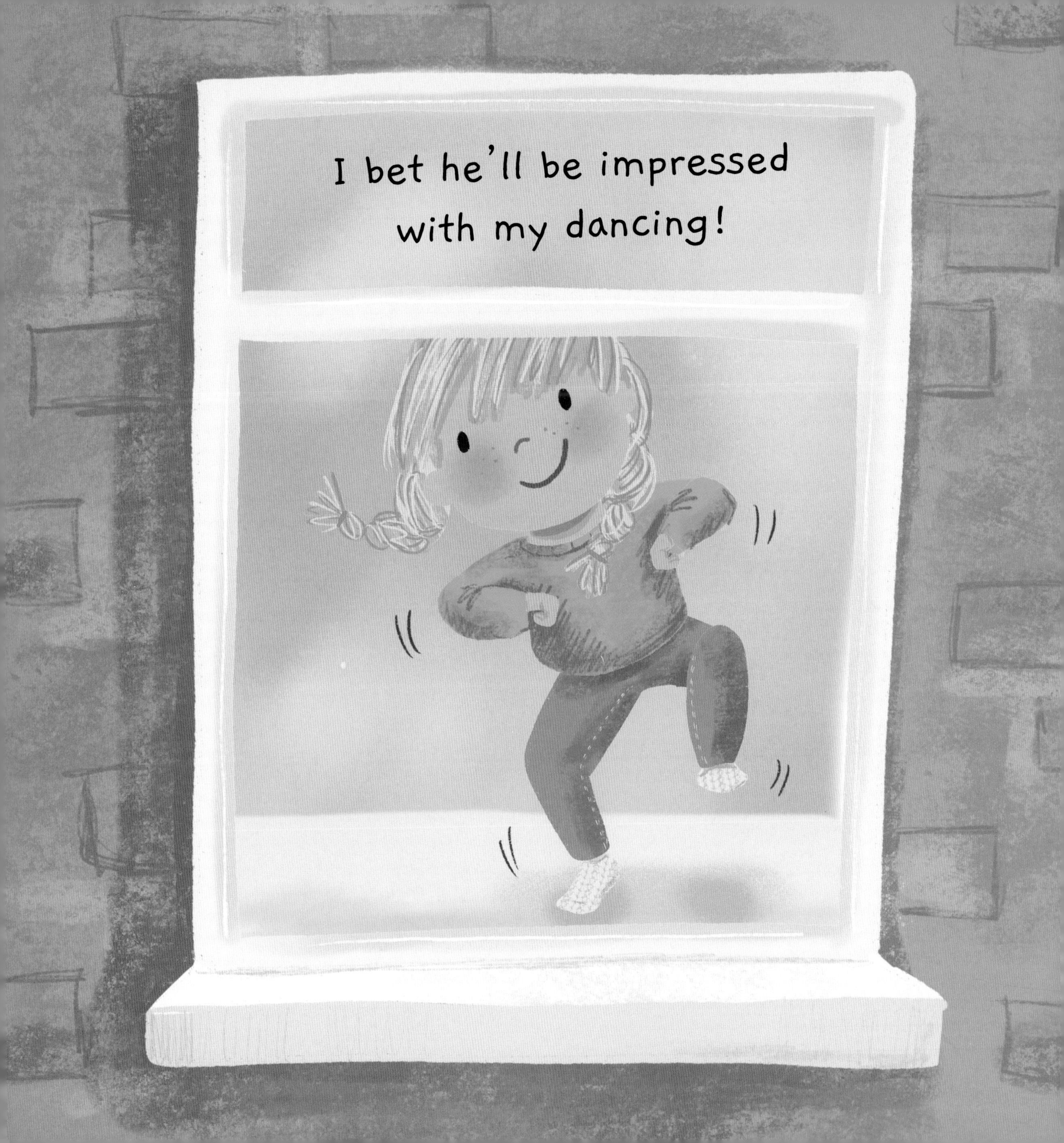
I bet he'll be impressed
with my dancing!

"Ha ha!"

"Hee hee!"

It's been a different sort of day,
finding new ways to have fun.

It may feel lonely sometimes, but...

...we are alone together.

Julia Seal

Julia is an author-illustrator from a small village in England. She knew from the age of five what she wanted to do for a living—draw pictures!

After studying Graphic Design and Illustration, Julia got a job making greeting cards, where she came home each day covered in glitter. After this, she managed to land her dream job of creating children's books, and hasn't looked back since. She's illustrated more than 70 books over the past 9 years!

Julia has recently started writing books and gets her inspiration from things going on around her. She keeps a little book of funny quotes and overheard snippets of conversations that often turn into stories. Her two children also provide endless inspiration.

Penguin Random House

Produced for DK by Collaborate Agency

Editor Sally Beets
US Editor Lori Hand
Designer Brandie Tully-Scott

Jacket Coordinator Issy Walsh
Publishing Manager Francesca Young
Publishing Director Sarah Larter
Production Editor Nikoleta Parasaki
Production Controller Ena Matagic

First American Edition, 2020
Published in the United States by DK Publishing
1450 Broadway, Suite 801, New York, NY 10018

A catalog record for this book
is available from the Library of Congress.
ISBN 978-0-7440-3668-8

DK books are available at special discounts when purchased in bulk for sales promotions, premiums, fund-raising, or educational use. For details, contact: DK Publishing Special Markets, 1450 Broadway, Suite 801, New York, NY 10018
SpecialSales@dk.com

Printed and bound in China

MIX
Paper from
responsible sources
FSC™ C018179

For the curious

www.dk.com